Learning to Read, Step by Step!

Ready to Read   Preschool–Kindergarten
• big type and easy words • rhyme and rhythm • picture clues
For children who know the alphabet and are eager to
begin reading.

Reading with Help   Preschool–Grade 1
• basic vocabulary • short sentences • simple stories
For children who recognize familiar words and sound out
new words with help.

Reading on Your Own   Grades 1–3
• engaging characters • easy-to-follow plots • popular topics
For children who are ready to read on their own.

Reading Paragraphs   Grades 2–3
• challenging vocabulary • short paragraphs • exciting stories
For newly independent readers who read simple sentences
with confidence.

Ready for Chapters   Grades 2–4
• chapters • longer paragraphs • full-color art
For children who want to take the plunge into chapter books
but still like colorful pictures.

STEP INTO READING® is designed to give every child a successful
reading experience. The grade levels are only guides; children will progress
through the steps at their own speed, developing confidence in their reading.
The F&P Text Level on the back cover serves as another tool to help you
choose the right book for your child.

Remember, a lifetime love of reading starts with a single step!

*This book is dedicated to
all the big people who are
helping smaller people
learn to read.
The StoryBots love you!*

Designed by Greg Mako

Copyright © 2017 by JibJab Bros. Studios

All rights reserved. Published in the United States by Random House Children's Books, a division of Penguin Random House LLC, New York.

Step into Reading, Random House, and the Random House colophon are registered trademarks of Penguin Random House LLC.

StoryBots® is a registered trademark of JibJab Bros. Studios.

Visit us on the Web!
StepIntoReading.com
randomhousekids.com

Educators and librarians, for a variety of teaching tools, visit us at RHTeachersLibrarians.com

ISBN 978-1-5247-1866-4 (trade) — ISBN 978-1-5247-1867-1 (lib. bdg.) — ISBN 978-1-5247-1868-8 (ebook)

Printed in the United States of America
10 9 8 7 6 5 4 3 2 1

This book has been officially leveled by using the F&P Text Level Gradient™ Leveling System.

STEP INTO READING®

STEP 1 READY TO READ

A SCIENCE READER

TYRANNOSAURUS REX

by Scott Emmons

illustrated by Nikolas Ilic and Eddie West

Random House 🏠 New York

I am Beep,
and this is Bo.

Back into
the past
we go!

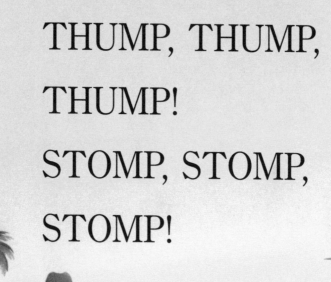

THUMP, THUMP, THUMP!
STOMP, STOMP, STOMP!

The T. rex hunts
for food to chomp!

See him prowl.

8

Hear him roar.

He is one BIG dinosaur!

His feet are huge.

He stands so tall!

Next to him,

we all look small.

He weighs a lot,
about eight tons.

The ground starts shaking
when he runs!

15

His legs are thick.

His tail is long.

My goodness,
he is really STRONG!

His arms do not reach
very far.
Just look how short
and thin they are.

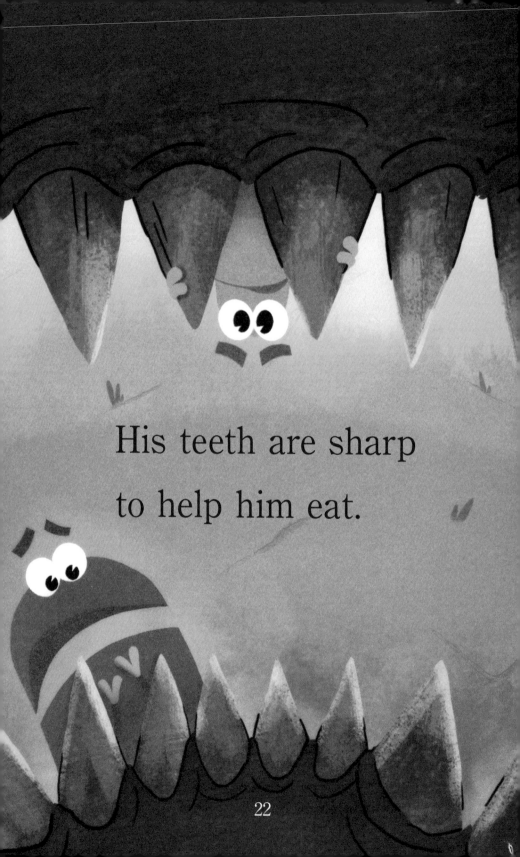

His teeth are sharp
to help him eat.

The food he likes to eat
is MEAT.

Smaller creatures
shake with fear.
They run and hide
when he is near.

And we run, too.
We have a hunch
he wants a StoryBot
for lunch!

We made it!

We are safe at last.

What luck that he
is not too fast!

TYRANNOSAURUS!

Look and see.

His name is BIG,

and so is he.

65,500,000 BC

31

Goodbye, T. rex!